SHADES OF LOVE

POETRY BOOK WITH THE DARKER SHADES OF THE FEELING WE CALL LOVE (MOSTLY)

SCARLA EVE

Copyright © Scarla Eve
All Rights Reserved.

This book has been self-published with all reasonable efforts taken to make the material error-free by the author. No part of this book shall be used, reproduced in any manner whatsoever without written permission from the author, except in the case of brief quotations embodied in critical articles and reviews.

The Author of this book is solely responsible and liable for its content including but not limited to the views, representations, descriptions, statements, information, opinions and references ["Content"]. The Content of this book shall not constitute or be construed or deemed to reflect the opinion or expression of the Publisher or Editor. Neither the Publisher nor Editor endorse or approve the Content of this book or guarantee the reliability, accuracy or completeness of the Content published herein and do not make any representations or warranties of any kind, express or implied, including but not limited to the implied warranties of merchantability, fitness for a particular purpose. The Publisher and Editor shall not be liable whatsoever for any errors, omissions, whether such errors or omissions result from negligence, accident, or any other cause or claims for loss or damages of any kind, including without limitation, indirect or consequential loss or damage arising out of use, inability to use, or about the reliability, accuracy or sufficiency of the information contained in this book.

Made with ♥ on the Notion Press Platform
www.notionpress.com

To those who love dark or tragic stories, despite knowing it'll just hurt them emotionally

And to those who occasionally enjoy normal romances because everyone is valid

Contents

Contents

Synopsis

The poetry book Shades of Love by Scarla Eve is about the different kinds of love people experience in their lives. Some of these may be relatable, and some may just be "Does this person need a hug?" since it mostly contains the deeper and sadder parts and stories of love that people experience, unfortunately. Some of these are based on my own experiences, but most of the poems in this have been inspired by songs or shows. Will you get the references?

Preface

I have always been more interested in stories that have sad or dark undertones. Poetry was just a beautiful way to present the feelings of those sad, monotone days to the confusing feelings about someone to the brutality that some people consider love. With this book, I want to show that love doesn't come in one shape or form. It can be beautiful, it can be tragic, it can be a mystery, and sometimes a nightmare.

I want to show that love in any form can be a story. Whether it is romantic, platonic, or self-love. I want people to see that they aren't alone in feeling a certain way and that even the most tragic stories can be beautiful and the most confusing feelings can make sense while not being clear.

About The Author

Latika Bhatt, aka Scarla Eve, is a 17-year-old girl from New Delhi, India. Spending most of her life reading books and watching game series online, she always found herself to be more attached to the characters than real people. So many concepts about life are still hard for her to comprehend but being able to write down these feelings has helped her understand a lot more than she could have anticipated. She always enjoyed the darker concepts of reality or stories, feeling more connected to characters that have a cruel fate rather than a happily ever after.

Acknowledgements

This is my first published book and I'm very happy to say that my friends and family were a HUGE help. I'm thankful to my friend, who is already an author - Paakhi Mittal, for being an influence on my writing journey. My actual poetry writing journey started with the diary she gave me on 31st October 2022.

I would like to thank all of my friends who inspired and encouraged me about my poems and story ideas. I don't think I would've made this book without their kind and instructive words.

I would like to thank my family who have always been supportive of my choices and the willingness they showed when I told them I was gonna publish my poems. I'm very grateful to them and their insights about my writing.

I would like to thank ALL the shows and songs that gave me ideas about my poems. I'm a huge fan of making theories, especially from music videos and writing from the different perspectives of characters in it. So yes, a big thanks to the internet for that I guess lol.

Also, I would like to thank Notion Press for allowing me to publish my book without any hassle. It was a smooth process and didn't require much from me, and publishing my first-ever book was a pleasant and interesting experience thanks to Notion Press.

1. Black Sorrow

Had I not met you,
I would've been long gone
Had I not met you,
I wouldn't have been such a foolish fawn
Making excuses until I realized
That your heart belonged to another
I knew that and my hope shattered
Seeing your eyes follow that pink feather
Freedom meant nothing if it wasn't with you
My heart drowning as I walked away from the gate
It was now up to you
The chord of my fate

We stand on the stage,
The crowd cheers in delight
And your face glaring at mine
My Black Sorrow,
Will you please be my demise?

2. Allen

Met him in a dream
His face was a blur but his voice was gentle
Crippling with fear on the shaky ground
He held out a hand and helped me out
I had never seen anyone like him
But something about that voice gave me comfort
Waking up the next day, he had not left my mind
That sweet voice lingering in my brain
Went to sleep and saw him again
But his face was no longer a blur
His hair was as white as a crystal
His eyes were a cyan color full of hope and trust
But somewhere I knew,
That the smile on his face was just the surface of the rust

3. Cellphone Love Story

The phone rang; we talked
It was my favorite sound, the ringing
The anticipation of hearing your voice
Made my heart flutter
I despise it; the ringing
Where are you now?
Was it my fault?
Do you hate me or love me?
Don't play this guessing game
The ringing continues and I feel my heart ache
The love I once felt, is now empty like your words
The room goes silent as my hands reach for the phone
My voice refuses to answer as the familiar voice is heard
"Hello?... Hello?..."

4. Leia

The one beyond the canvas
Using the brush to color my world
Your eyes are out of focus
Your voice unheard
The dullness of your eyes
Don't match the sparkle in mine
So move me with those lies
As I treat you like a shrine
Purify this stagnant heart
Bury this lie of a canvas
Call out my name so we never part
Make me your reality so you can finally pass
If I can't leave behind the proof of us two
What am I meant to do with this warmth?
Engrave me like a fool
And end me for all I was worth

5. Young Love

How could this happen?
Why did this happen?
To think that you of all people are on my mind
To think you are the one from who my feelings cannot hide
I was too young and naive to realize
That you were there in front of my eyes
Covering those feelings with banter and hate
I failed to realize that it might be fate
You approached me as a joke
Which resulted in years of friendship
Are we even friends?
How will I ever know what you feel for me?
Your presence is more than enough to make my day
But in the end, my feelings remain in vain
It's not possible for us to be
But I still long for the day when you feel the same for me

6. Love = Everything?

The most important thing in life
Colored by the delusion of being pretty
Someone's husband or someone's wife
In the end, all they hear is pity
Their eyes are empty; unlike the ocean
Their smile makes your heart weep
Become a part of the commotion
Don't be afraid to fall deep
You don't need to think
Just follow your heart
I know you want to blink
But you know it will tear you apart
The most important thing in life
Give up everything for it
The drama love will provide
Will cost you nothing but your sanity for it

7. Galleria

Standing together in this desolate room
What should've been our Galleria
Lies the blood of my heart
And your empty apologies chanted like a mantra
Please give me a beautiful life,
The one that I dreamt of
Please put down the gun
It was foolish to save our love
Now all I have in my mind is 'Run, run, run'
I wish I could turn back time
To a life full of love and hope
Don't stop breathing, my dear
Your words can't be washed away with soap
Your blood runs cold
Are you already dead or just dreaming?
As if you have a thought in that mold
But you can't leave,
This house isn't nearly as cold
Please give me a life,
As normal as it can be
I have nothing in the afterlife
All that is left is the tower of my corrupted fantasy

You ruined what could've been
Now pay the price for a millennia
Standing alone in this desolate room
What should've been our Galleria

8. Stay By My Side

Looking at that face,

Something burns inside

Hearing that name

The heart forms a smile

Why is it that you say my name so often?

Why is it that whenever you see me you smile?

Am I overanalyzing?

Could it be just that you treat everyone the same?

The words that leave your lips

Go over my head but still somehow reach my heart

An idiot is what I call myself,

Yet you don't hesitate to speak to me and treat me like I'm a part

I don't care if it's a friendly gesture,

The way my heart jumps

When your hand holds my shoulder,

My mind always tells me otherwise

Stay by my side

So I can hear you every day

Stay by my side

I'll keep you in every way

Who knows what reality holds

As long as you are there

I wouldn't ask for more

9. A Fighter

Known to be a fighter
Nothing brought you down
Your smile was like a flower
It wasn't meant to be
Or maybe it was?
Tell me now, why are you quiet?
My hands on your body
My fists hitting your chest
Maybe you weren't invincible after all…

10. Shameless Animal

Your voice rings like a melody
Your back against the wall
The hands on your neck
Being the only thing keeping you steady
Burning skin and muffled voices
A sin? So be it
The coldness of your fingers brings me closer
If I were to die now
At least I'd as your lover
The moon reflects in my eyes
As I stare out the window
The single bed feels empty
And my heart hollow
Ah… what a cruel and shameless creature is the human mind.

11. Look My Way

Destined to the throne
My interest in people was not important
Written scriptures gave me more love
Than the ones who called me their own
A day to celebrate
Or so I thought
Once again,
My future was decided
But… then there was you.
The skin of an imp
The confidence of a devil
You made my heart jump
As we ran around like foolish children
Where are you now?
How did we fall apart…
We weren't close to begin with, were we?
But please, see me before you go
Status, Money
Fuck that
Just let me love you,
Properly this time
This heart of a foolish owl,

Take it away so I can't shout
Look my way and help me remember,
The times when our laughter would silence the crowd

• 14 •

12. My Cure

The feather is gone
The light in your eyes, the hope in your voice
All vanished as you sing now
They are watching us, Love
Don't make a scene out loud
The hope you kept,
I cannot replace it
You chose your peace
I'll keep mine like the last bid
Your eyes always searched,
They only looked at mine when your fist met my jaw
Bruises were nothing when your attention was mine
So, darling, I'll keep doing the same until the end of time
Your anger, your blood
It was gorgeous, it was delicious
At least something of yours was mine
You are my only cure,
The one that will kill me
The one who will live
So, forgive me just this once
One Last Kiss
One last goodbye

I have no one to miss
So let me put on this show and comply
Never thought I'd be happy
to wrap my hands around your throat
As the scoreboard showed our vote
You had won… but you aren't fighting me anymore
Seeing the acceptance in your eyes made me shake
You didn't even fight it, despite not knowing what I was
planning
You just closed your eyes and waited to break
Look at me one last time, please…
It wasn't until the pain reached my heart
That I felt blood pouring down my lips
I'm so relieved…
You were safe Till my end at least
You stand on the stage,
Blood seeping through my clothes and under your feet
My Black Sorrow
You became my demise like it was meant to be

13. Left but Not Forgotten

A simple action
A simple word
Living beings strive to experience it
Just once, whether as a friend or a partner
Years go by and the feeling remains
Hairs are white and you can barely walk
Yet the face of those who remained,
They make you want to wait
What is it about them that makes things seem easy?
Why does your heart ache at the thought of them leaving?
Emotions are confusing,
But it makes sense with them
You cannot deny it,
Even if they anger you or upset you
No matter how hard you try
You cannot deny the love you feel for them and why
Can't be friends but can't be strangers either
Why must I feel like such?
You smile and I feel hurt
I guess it was true,

To the ones who were here before us
It's all said and done
I laugh, "You don't outgrow Love."

14. Too Late

That smile I saw
One without mockery or hate
I didn't realize
It was only to hide your pain
Running to your house
The rain covers my feet with mud
Grabbing a rock,
For some reason
I knew you weren't gonna answer
Was it my fault;
For not picking up the phone?
I cannot think otherwise
As my arms hold your body
In this room all alone

15. Blue

Blue has always been my favorite color
Its presence is calm like the sky
Dark as the night
Peaceful as the rain
I see no flaws in it, no matter how hard I try
It can be monotone and gloomy
But even then the beauty remains
Just like the color blue
I see no flaw in you
You are perfect in every way
Even when life doesn't work well for you at times
I am captivated by you
Just like blue
I wish I could shout your name
Tell my feelings for the world to hear
But I can only do as much as talk nice and be there
Because life isn't like a re-do game
If only you were just the color blue.

16. Not Communicative

Whenever you are down
You seek me
Whenever you are high
You indulge me
Where does one find comfort,
The way you find it with me?
Where is that trust in you
Which I fail to see?
How do you make it look easy
Like I'm the one who is weird
Can't I reach out for help
Without feeling tongue-tied or fear?

17. A Letter From Melancholy

You see that face in the mirror
How still and lifeless it is
Thoughts that have no exterior
They don't know what they miss
"I'm okay" is what you tell yourself and the others
Then why is it that you hear the birds chirping at 5 AM?
Your hands are shaking and your heart cries
Others may be fooled but I am a part of you, my dear
The dull days become comforting
The self-hate becomes your home
The memories of the past start lingering
Every time you speak, the sadness is evident in your tone
I have existed for centuries
Millions have lost their lives because of me
But I believe that you, my dear
Are far stronger than many
Let out your heart
And embrace the hurt
Because I will always be there
You will be okay,

And live to fight the world and its snare

• 23 •

18. Weapon With A Heart

A weapon raised to be human
The emptiness in those ocean eyes
Held no remorse
For the ones she unalived
Coming from nowhere
She finally found a place
The mind of a soldier
Yet she cried at his name
The bullets pierced her arms
Defeating her only purpose
To one she was worthless
To one she was the world
"I love you" the words foreign to her
But he told her anyway
She could only cry
Screaming at him to explain
The warmth of her hands
No longer to be felt
Yet the words they type
Are enough to be held

SCARLA EVE

Looking at the sky
She searched for his face
In hopes of telling him
She finally knew what "Love" meant
And will continue to live for his grace

19. Jealousy? Who she?

Even though you aren't mine
Seeing you laughing and smiling with another
It makes me want to hide you away
It's stupid to want that smile for myself
But it hurts to see you treating me like anyone else
You don't know
You will never know
How badly I want to keep you and make you happy
But I'm not the one
I can never be the one for anyone; let alone you
I'm not someone who usually gets jealous
But I'll be damned to know you like another
You're laughing with them,
Such a sweet voice
How dare I want to keep it for myself
Jealousy is infuriating, isn't it?

20. Pathetic Doll

Medication? Therapy?
Love? Instability?
Love isn't like this
Yet I feel my face heat
Why doesn't my heart ache at your words?
I should hate this, hate you
That sweet voice of yours
Makes the insults feel like honey
Your hatred fuels my heart
Your words lock me
I'm burnt and hurt
But I wouldn't let go of this for any key
Look at me with those hateful eyes
Break me, be harsh
Keep your eyes on me
And call me "Pathetic" once again
Because when it comes to you,
I'm nothing but a pathetic doll, my dear.

21. The Heart's Feeling

Confusion is one way to describe it
My brain does not understand
Nothing seems to match your wit
And I find myself at the palm of your hand
You don't speak
Yet I understand every word
When you speak
I wonder if anything more beautiful can be heard
My smiles are content
The ones my heart cannot fake
Happiness is usually just a concept
Until I hear the familiar voice rise into wake
My back against the wall
Hands to my face, hiding away from the crowd
How frustrating can a person be,
While also being the one you cannot live without?
There is no definite way to describe it
Losing your senses because of another mere being
I could write paragraphs to try and decipher it
But no one is smart enough for a heart and it's feeling

22. Coin Locker Baby

The night we shared
The love we harbored
We were too young
Into the locker, it goes
People after people
One oughta slip
Another mistake
Into the locker, it goes
Is it love or a chore?
Erasing the mistakes of every night
The trash piles on
But the bone-crushing goes deaf, even to a fly
Somebody oughta find you
Before your body gets blue
Because I cannot come back
As I have forgotten all about you
Goodbye, goodbye
As a new one comes to life
Goodbye, goodbye
My coin locker baby
The one who never got to cry

23. The Star I Lost

"Stars are the ones who left too soon."
You said, your lips held a smile
But your eyes were dull
I knew you wanted to join them too
"Stars are prettier than the moon."
You said with a laugh
You had no idea, dear
That your sound could brighten any room
"Stars live forever, you fool…"
How could you lie with that smile?
Holding onto your hand, your blood ran cold
My star, you left me too soon

24. Hitogawari

The sun casts down warmly
It was a day to remember
The first time you smiled at me
My heart was full, knowing you were my forever
A mistake on my part?
The ring that once was full of love
Now laid heavy on my heart
Makeup cannot hide this
Guess I'll stay in my room
Oh, you brought bandages?
How sweet of you…
Why ask for forgiveness
When you do it all over again?
Don't trouble yourself like this
My nails have already removed the pain
Don't call me your love
The bandages are nothing but a web
You want to kiss me?
Then drench your lips in red

25. Blink Gone

Do you think I never noticed?

The stares you gave me across the room

The smiles that never missed

I did not know what to make of it,

Until you kissed me and I saw your grave

I have no one left

It was inevitable on this stage

But to think you let me live

I don't know whether to feel guilt or hate

Why didn't you just tell me?

Instead of ruining my flower crowns

I know I was fixated on the feather

But maybe that night I wouldn't have turned around

You couldn't even bring yourself to say "I want you"

So why bother when I want to depart this life?

You got your last kiss, Ivan

But who gave you the right?

Your blood soaked through my feet

The cheers of the crowd are born

I don't know whether to shout or weep

In a blink, you're gone

And now I'm left with the guilt to keep

26. Hell's Pride

You can forgive my sins
Or change my fate
But he won't return my wings
Or open the gate
Do you know every corner?
Know every fear?
You, humans, do not concur
But run all the same from the slightest noise you hear
Those images in your mind
Those pictures you see
I do not look like Hell's Pride
I do not have a sad backstory
Romanticize me all you want
Change my story and my name
Preachers are foolish with their taunt
Who would tell them it'll all be in vain?
Humans seek comfort so I'll be it
Now why do you show me that fear?
It's not something to be easily forgotten
That the devil wrapped in silk is still the devil, my dear.

27. Killed Someone For You

A crime was committed
Taking someone's life was frowned upon
The sirens could not be missed
I know I should run
But my will was far agone
I long to hear your voice
I need a place to hide
Yes, it was my choice
I will explain if you let me stay the night
I've practiced my confession
I won't make a mistake this time
Don't send me back to that prison
If the blood is my own, is it really a crime?
They ask why I did it
As I lay on the white sheet
Bandaging the crimson slit
All I heard were your last words on repeat
I completed every task you gave me
So what's the point of living?
I hope you are waiting for me

Because next time I'm not coming back
And you are not abandoning me

28. I Told You So

Your hair flows like a river

Your eyes sparkle with love

You could kiss a hundred thousand boys, my dear

But I know you will always be my dove

Since when did love have rules?

Or is that just an excuse to not seem shallow?

Go ahead and follow those crudes

I won't say "I told you so."

Sleeping beside the one you now call your lover

Until he gets up for work at five

He doesn't look at you and think "I love her"

You both know you are nothing more than his wife

Now that you think about me

Does your heart still stutter?

I hate to say "I told you so" with such glee

But how can I not,

When you finally say "I love her" but it's too late to set your heart

free

29. Don't Look Away

It started as a deal
One night to survive the next three
It was all just for your appeal
Now you act like a hero by saying "I set you free"?
Don't say you understand
When I talk about my pain
You had it all in hand
Even before you got on this train
How is it fair,
To think that your love is more than a decoy?
Because as far as I'm aware,
I'm no better than the servants you employ
You say "Let's make amends"
Like it's a promise among children
You used me for months on end
Am I supposed to be smitten?
Don't look away
Now that you are faced with your mistakes
Look my way
I don't care how much your heart aches
Leave no room for sorrow
Throw it away and drown your fears

Because unlike me,
"Your Highness" doesn't shed tears
And will thrive again while drowning in his misery

• 38 •

30. Shades Of Love

Hearing heartbeats from the womb
The smiles shared across the room
Holding his hand in the hospital bed
The newly found peace is finally held
Countless days spent in solitude
To finding hope within the faded hue
Holding your own hand for comfort
Replaced by a hug after every meet-up
There is no such thing as insignificance
Since those actions leave larger marks
What seemed like a normal hug to you
Was the first form of love someone got in that class
The stars in the sky
As they walk with you with a flash
Studying together,
Interrupted by laughter because of a mispronounced word or a
dash
Realizing that affection isn't the same for all
Because of different experiences and beliefs of the above
Leave questions that we cannot answer at all
So why bother,
When you can just appreciate the different shades of love

Final Words

Thank you for reading Shades Of Love, I hope it was a satisfactory experience for you. If you have any suggestions, want to ask questions, or give reviews to me directly, please contact me through my email - scarlaeve@gmail.com.

The Next book will be based on urban legends or horror scenarios in general. So, if you enjoy that kind of content, I hope I meet your expectations since I'm a huge fan of the horror genre myself.

Until we meet again, fellow readers.

www.ingramcontent.com/pod-product-compliance
Lightning Source LLC
Chambersburg PA
CBHW031243130726
47988CB00008B/3217